What's Going on Down There?

What's Going on Down There?

Answers to Questions Boys Find Hard to Ask

Karen Gravelle
with Nick and Chava Castro

Illustrations by Robert Leighton

Walker and Company
New York

40409

Without the help of the men and boys who shared their thoughts and experiences about puberty with me, this book would have been much shorter and a lot less interesting. Thank you all! Thanks also to Dr. Ingeborg Schraft-Hoffman and Dr. Radoslav Jovanovic for their assistance.

First published in the United States of America in 1998
by Walker Publishing Company, Inc.

Published simultaneously in Canada
by Thomas Allen & Son Canada, Limited, Markham, Ontario

Library of Congress Cataloging-in-Publication Data
Gravelle, Karen.
What's going on down there?: Answers to questions boys find hard to ask/Karen Gravelle, with Nick and Chava Castro; illustrations by Robert Leighton.
p.   cm   Includes index.
Summary: Describes the physical and emotional changes that occur in boys (and, to a lesser extent, in girls) during puberty and discusses sexual activity, homosexuality, AIDS, and other related topics.
ISBN 0-8027-8671-5 —ISBN 0-8027-7540-3 (paperback)
1. Teenage boys—Physiology—Juvenile literature. 2. Puberty—Juvenile literature. 3. Sex instruction for boys—Juvenile literature [1. Puberty. 2. Sex instruction for boys.]
I. Castro, Nick. II. Castro, Chava. III. Leighton, Robert, illustrator.
IV. Title.
RJ143.G73   1998
612.6'61—dc21   98–3686
CIP
AC

Book design by Dede Cummings

Printed in the United States of America

4 6 8 10 9 7 5

Contents

A Note from Karen
with Nick and Chava

Since I'm not a guy, I wasn't sure exactly what concerns boys who are going through puberty might have. So I decided to ask some experts—thirteen-year-old Chava Castro and his eleven-year-old brother, Nick. Chava and Nick both had sex education in their school, but they felt that many of their questions didn't get answered. There were other things they wondered about but didn't want to bring up in public. Therefore, they thought a book like this was a very good idea and agreed to help me write it. Here's what they had to say about working on *What's Going on Down There?*

Chava: I really had fun working on this book, and I learned a lot! In my sex education class, the teacher never told us (and the books didn't either) that you can't ejaculate and urinate at the same time. That was not a good thing to leave out! I was really worried about this until I finally asked my mom. It was also a relief to learn that guys have emotional times during puberty and that I wasn't weird for feeling this way. This book will be great to read in private, because I'd be *really* embarrassed to ask questions in class. Everyone would laugh or tease me for sure!

Nick: I liked helping to write this book because sex ed in the fifth grade didn't explain enough about my body. I'm lucky that my mom is a nurse, but by working on the book I thought of things that I forgot to ask her that have confused me sometimes. Asking your friends isn't always the best way to find out, because they can have some strange information sources. At least now I know that all guys go through these changes, not just me.

What's Going on Down There?

Introduction

If you're a boy somewhere between ten and fourteen years old, you probably don't need a book to tell you that your body is starting to change. Even if you haven't noticed much of a difference in yourself yet, chances are you've seen changes occurring in some of your friends.

For example, guys who used to be your height may suddenly have gotten much taller than you—or perhaps you're the one who's now towering over the other boys in your class. Some of you may have noticed that your shoulders are getting broader and your whole body seems more muscular. For the first time, dark hairs may be starting to grow under your arms and on your lips. Most of the time, boys your age look forward to these changes or at least feel OK about them.

But other changes may not be so great, which is one reason that some boys wonder if growing up is such a good thing. A lot of guys begin to develop bumps on their faces, and there isn't a person alive who likes having pimples. Or, right in the middle of a normal conversation, your voice may suddenly become high and squeaky.

These changes—both the ones you want and the ones you don't—are things that other people can see. But some of the most important changes are ones that only you are likely to notice. For example, around age eleven or twelve, give or take a little, a boy's penis begins to look different, feel different, and even act different.

What's Going on Down There? will help you understand all of these changes—what causes them, when to expect them, and how to handle those that concern you. All of these changes are connected; they all have to do with the fact that you are becoming a man. So let's start with the things that make you a male in the first place.

CHAPTER 1

Your Body

The things that make a person male or female have to do with reproduction, or having children. Therefore, these differences involve the genital, or sexual, organs—the parts of the body that make it possible for a person to reproduce.

As you probably know, it takes both a man and a woman to create a baby. That's because half the instructions necessary to form a baby's body come from the man and half from the woman. These instructions are contained in a man's sperm and in a woman's eggs. A sperm and an egg must unite inside a woman's body for a baby to develop. We'll talk about how all this happens in chapter 6. But right now, let's concentrate on your genitals, the organs that make you a male.

The Genitals

Some of a boy's genitals, such as his penis and testicles, are easy to see because they are large and placed out in the open. But you also have several internal reproductive organs that you probably haven't been aware of. All of your genital organs, whether they are inside or outside your body, play a part in making you able to have children.

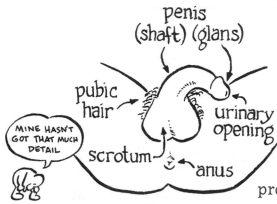

penis
(shaft) (glans)

pubic
hair

urinary
opening

scrotum

anus

MINE HASN'T
GOT THAT MUCH
DETAIL

Testicles and Scrotum

The testicles are two nut-shaped organs that hang in a sac of wrinkly skin between a male's legs. Their job is to produce sperm. Sperm are tiny cells that look like little tadpoles—if you could see them, that is. Sperm are so small they're

4

visible only through a microscope. Like tad-poles, they have tails that enable them to swim.

The sac that contains the testicles is called the scrotum. Since young boys don't have sperm, their testicles and scrotum are small. But as a boy be-gins to become a man, these organs start to grow and his testicles begin to make sperm.

You may be wondering how sperm get from a sac between a man's legs into a woman's body. This is where the penis and internal sexual organs come in.

Penis

You already know a lot about your penis. It's the part of your body that you use to urinate, or pee. But the penis serves another purpose as well. It plays a very important role in being able to have children, because it provides a way for a man's sperm to leave his body and enter a woman's body. The penis is also the source of most of the pleasurable feelings a male experiences when he has sex.

Of course, sperm first have to get from the tes-ticles to the penis.

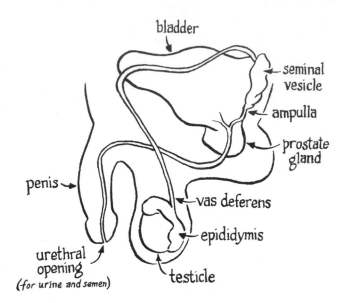

bladder

seminal vesicle

ampulla

prostate gland

penis

vas deferens

epididymis

urethral opening
(for urine and semen)

testicle

From the Testicles to the Penis

There are several internal tubes and organs that connect the testicles to the penis. At the top of each testicle is an organ called the epididymis (eh-pih-DIH-dih-miss). Sperm go from the testicles, where they are made, to the epididymis, where they mature, or grow up. Once they have matured, they travel through another tube, the vas deferens (VAS DEF-eh-renz), to a sort of holding tank called the ampulla (am-POOL-ah), where they are stored. Luckily, the vas deferens has muscles to help push the sperm along. At this point in their lives, sperm are not very energetic swimmers and couldn't get from the epididymis to the ampulla on their own.

Near the ampulla are two other organs, the seminal vesicles and the prostate gland. They provide fluids that give the sperm energy and help them travel through the penis. At the ampulla, the vas deferens connects with the urethra. The urethra is the tube inside your penis. It's the same tube that urine travels through when you pee.

Circumcised or Uncircumcised

All baby boys are born with similar genitals. Shortly after birth, however, some parents choose to have their sons circumcised. You can tell whether you have been circumcised by looking at

Circumcised   Uncircumcised

Foreskin

your penis. Some boys have loose skin at the end of the penis that slides back to uncover the tip of the penis. This loose skin is called the foreskin. If you still have a foreskin, you haven't been circumcised.

Other boys are missing this skin. It was removed, or circumcised, shortly after they were born. If the tip of your penis is always uncovered, you have been circumcised. Whether you have a foreskin or not makes no difference in how your penis works. Both types of penises—circumcised and uncircumcised—work in exactly the same way and equally well.

You may be wondering why some parents decide to have their sons circumcised and whether it hurts when the foreskin is cut off. Boys from Jewish or Muslim families are circumcised for religious reasons. But other boys may be circumcised too. Circumcision helps prevent germs from collecting under the foreskin. Thus, in the past, many boys were circumcised to prevent disease. With careful and regular washing, however, the area under the foreskin can be kept clean, so fewer boys are circumcised for health reasons today.

Since circumcision is done when a boy is a very young baby, older boys and men who have been circumcised don't remember whether it hurt or not. Babies cry when they are being circumcised, so we know it must hurt them to some degree. But circumcision takes only a few minutes, and babies stop crying as soon as it's over. Therefore, we know the pain doesn't last very long.

CHAPTER 2

Body Changes

All of the changes discussed in this book have something in common. In one way or another, they are designed to help you grow from a child into a man who can have and take care of children of your own. The time in a child's life when the body goes through these changes is called puberty. In boys, puberty starts somewhere between ages ten and fourteen and is completed around ages sixteen to eighteen.

Genital Changes

Since puberty is basically about reproduction, it naturally involves the genital, or sexual, organs.

Early Changes

Throughout childhood, your genitals have continued to grow. But while they've gotten a little bigger as you've gotten older, they haven't changed much in appearance from year to year.

However, as a boy enters puberty, special chemicals called hormones begin to tell the body to grow in a different way. Hormones are produced by the brain and other organs, and they guide sexual development in both boys and girls. The main hormone responsible for development in boys is called testosterone.

In response to the signals these hormones send out, a boy's genitals not only start to grow at a much faster rate but also begin to change. The first thing that most boys notice is that their testicles are becoming larger and their scrotum is starting to hang lower. However, instead of growing similarly, the two testicles now begin to look different from each other. One testicle starts to become a little larger and hang lower than the other.

If you don't know that this is normal, seeing one testicle getting bigger and sagging below the other can be upsetting. Boys often worry that the bigger one has become diseased or that the smaller one isn't going to grow any more.

There is a good reason why one testicle begins to drop below the other. As you probably know from experience, it hurts a lot when your testicles get hit or crushed. If they continued to grow side by side, there wouldn't be room between your legs for both testicles as they got larger. When you walked, they could easily get squished together, which would be very painful. But with one testicle hanging below the other, this doesn't happen.

You also don't need to worry if one testicle becomes a little larger than the other. Often, the testicle that hangs lower also grows more quickly. With time, the other testicle will catch up, and they will both be about the same size when you are fully developed. As you go through puberty, your testicles may even change positions, so that the testicle that started out higher ends up hanging lower than the other.

At the same time that the testicles begin to grow, the skin on the scrotum becomes baggier, wrinklier, and darker. The penis, on the other hand, doesn't change much initially.

Although these early changes generally begin when a boy is around eleven or twelve years old, some boys enter puberty a year or so earlier, whereas others start a year or so later. Just because a boy begins puberty at a younger age doesn't mean that he will grow up to be more manly than someone who starts later, or even that he will finish maturing first.

Moving Along

As a boy gets a little older, his penis also begins to grow more rapidly, getting both longer and wider. The testicles and scrotum keep on getting larger too, and all three genital organs become even darker in color. Your genitals will continue to grow until your penis measures from three and a half to four and a half inches long and your testicles are about one and three-quarter inches long. Of course, some young men will be a little bigger than this, and some a little smaller. In general, boys' genitals reach their full growth around age sixteen, but many boys are a year or so younger or a year or so older when this happens.

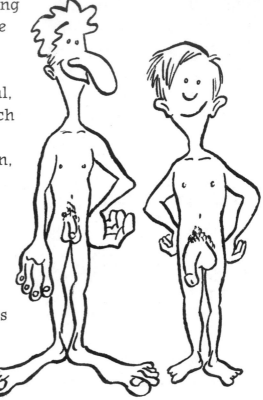

Speaking of penis size, chances are you've heard jokes about men who have "little dicks" or even exaggerated tales of others who have huge penises. You may also have heard that men from particular racial or ethnic groups have larger penises than men from other groups. Or that you can tell what size a man's penis is by the size of his feet, his nose, or some other body part. If you're like a lot of boys, you may have occasionally tried to sneak a peek at your friends' penises to see how yours compares. This is certainly understandable. After all, given the constant talk about penis size, who can blame you for being worried that your penis will be too small?

But before you get all caught up in how large your penis will eventually be, let's take a look at the facts. First, smaller penises work just as well as larger ones. Second, in preparation for having sex, all penises get larger and become stiff, or erect. (We'll talk more about erections in chapter 3.) But when this happens, smaller penises tend to increase more in size than larger ones. That means that differences in penis size generally even out when men have sex. Penis size also has nothing to do with how many children a man can have or how easily he can make a woman pregnant. Finally, contrary to what you may have heard, penis size has nothing to do with whether females will be attracted to you or how much you will be able to please them sexually. So if penis size doesn't make a difference, what difference does it make if yours is smaller or larger? The answer is— none!

By the way, racial or ethnic background has nothing to do with penis size. And no one can guess the size of your penis by looking at your feet, your nose, or anything else. (If that were possible, men would be very self-conscious about showing their feet or noses in public.)

More Hair

Another change that you can expect is the appearance of hair where it's never been before—on your face, under your arms, and usually on your chest. In some boys, hair also begins to grow on the shoulders, back, or stomach. And almost every boy finds the hair on his arms and legs getting thicker and darker.

While this hair is visible to everyone, the very first new hairs are likely to show up where no one but you can see them—around the base of your penis. This is pubic hair, and for a few boys it is the first sign of puberty. However, in most guys, pubic hair doesn't develop until after the testicles have begun to grow.

As a boy matures, his pubic hair spreads from the base of the penis to the scrotum and to a triangular area on the lower abdomen just above the penis. In some boys, pubic hair also appears on the inner thighs. And it can even grow in a line up to the navel, or belly button.

If the hair on your head is straight or light in color, you may be surprised to see that your pubic hair looks quite different. Regardless of the texture and color of hair on the rest of your body, your pubic hair will generally be darker and curlier.

Unlike pubic hair, a boy's facial hair doesn't usually begin to appear until his genitals are fairly well developed. So most boys are somewhere between fourteen and sixteen when they first notice the beginnings of a mustache. Hair around the sideburns and on the chin begins to come in a little later. Like pubic hair, beards and mustaches are often a different color from the hair on a boy's head, particularly if he is a blond or redhead. About the time that you start developing facial hair, hair will begin to grow under your arms as well.

The new hair developing on your body and face is one thing connected with puberty that can continue changing even after you're sexually mature. For example, some young men don't get their full amount of pubic hair until they are twenty

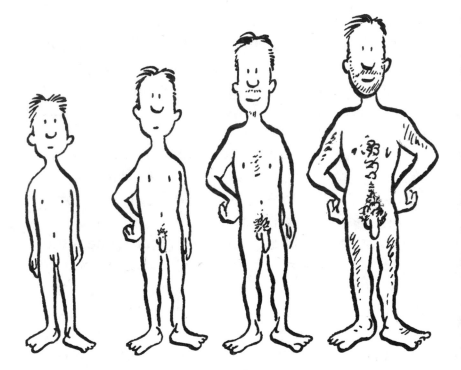

WHAT'S GOING ON DOWN THERE?

years old. And other men find their beard is still getting thicker when they are thirty!

Although there isn't any way to predict how much hair you will have on your body and your face, the amount you will develop is partially determined by your race. In general, Caucasian, or white, men tend to have the most hair, whereas Asian or Native American men have the least. Men of African descent usually fall somewhere in between.

Many boys look forward to shaving the hair on their face as part of becoming a man. Others shave because their mustache and beard have not yet filled out, and they feel their facial hair looks scraggly and unattractive. Since shaving facial hair tends to make it grow back somewhat darker and thicker, some boys may shave in an attempt to make this hair more noticeable. Other boys have no intention of shaving their mustache or beard. They are proud of their facial hair and like the way it looks.

Whether you decide to shave or not is totally up to you. But if you do start shaving, be sure to use a blade that is clean and free of nicks. And take special care when shaving around pimples, because accidentally cutting them can cause further infection and scarring. Using soap or shaving cream on your face can help the razor glide more smoothly over your skin and makes shaving easier and more comfortable.

African-American boys (or other men with very tightly curled facial hairs) may develop bumps on the skin as a result of shaving, particularly under the chin and on the neck. These razor bumps, as they are called, are not pimples but tiny ingrown hairs. As these hairs grow out, the bumps will disappear. If you are bothered by razor bumps, using a razor that cuts the hair at the skin's surface, not beneath it, will help to prevent this problem.

Getting Taller and More Muscular

Have you noticed how girls who used to be your height have suddenly shot up to become the tallest kids in your class? This rapid increase in height is called the growth spurt, and it's one of the first signs of puberty in girls. Boys go through a growth spurt too, but theirs usually starts a few years later, when they are about thirteen or fourteen. So for a couple of years until they catch up, boys tend to be shorter than girls.

There's a good reason it's called a growth spurt. Once it starts, boys (and girls) begin to grow at a much faster rate than when they were younger. Most children grow about two inches taller each year. But once the growth spurt begins, the average boy grows three and a half inches a year, and some boys add as much as a whopping five inches in one year! The growth spurt lasts for a couple of years, and then growth slows down again. But most boys keep growing at this slower rate until they are twenty.

Arms, legs, and especially feet grow particularly fast. Boys whose feet start growing before the rest of their body often worry that their feet will continue nonstop, growing totally out of proportion. Fortunately, your feet are generally the first part of your body to quit growing, so by the time your growth spurt is over, your limbs and torso will have caught up.

Along with getting taller, a boy's body also becomes more muscular. The shape of the body begins to change as well. The shoulders broaden and the chest becomes more developed—changes most guys really look forward to!

Speaking of chests—something else can happen that you probably won't be as thrilled about. At some point during puberty, most boys find their breasts becoming swollen and sore. In some cases, the swelling can be quite noticeable. If you aren't aware that this is normal *and temporary*, suddenly seeing yourself developing breasts "like a girl" is almost guaranteed to upset you. The lumps, swelling, and soreness will go away with time, but it

may take a year or so. In the meantime, try to be patient. Remember, a lot of other guys are going through this too, even if they don't admit it.

Pimples

While most boys look forward to becoming taller and more muscular or seeing the beginnings of a mustache, some of the skin changes that occur with puberty are less welcome. Pimples, for example, are one development no one is happy about.

During puberty, the oil glands in the skin become more active, producing greater amounts of

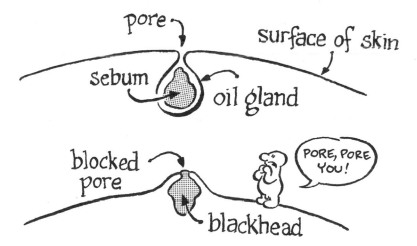

oil, or sebum. When this oil clogs a pore in the skin, it causes a blackhead. If the clogged pore gets inflamed or infected, a pimple results. Pimples can range from occasional bumps on the forehead, nose, or chin to a full-scale case of severe acne that covers the face and sometimes extends to the shoulders, back, and chest.

Since it's extremely rare for anyone—boy or girl—to go through puberty without ever developing pimples, it's good to know how to deal with them.

The best way to prevent pores in your skin from becoming clogged with oil and infected is to keep your skin clean. That way, there is less chance that oil will build up on the surface of your skin and if it does, less chance that there is bacteria around to cause infection.

Keeping your skin clean means thoroughly washing your face in the morning and before you go to bed. It also means keeping your hair clean. The increase in oil produced by your oil glands makes your hair more oily too. And greasy or dirty hair that touches your face adds extra oil and bacteria to your skin. Since pimples can also break out on the shoulders and back, you should keep these areas clean as well.

If you're like many guys, you may be tempted to try to pop pimples when they appear. This is a bad idea, because popping pimples can result in perma- nent scars. How-

LOOK OUT— SHE'S GONNA BLOW!

ever, knowing this doesn't seem to stop most kids. Therefore, if you are going to pop a pimple, at least wash your hands and the area around the pimple first. That way, you may keep the pimple from becoming even more infected.

Although keeping your skin clean is a must, it often isn't enough. If you wash carefully but are still bothered by pimples, there are a number of products you can buy in a drugstore that will help you control them. However, if you have serious acne, even these products may not do the job.

Having a bad case of acne is no joke. It can make you feel extremely unattractive and self-conscious. It can also lead to scarring, even after the acne is gone. Although pimples and acne are usually a thing of the past once your body has fully matured, that can take years. In the meantime, the fact that the problem will be gone when you're twenty isn't much of a help. That's why it's good to know that there are special doctors called dermatologists who can treat acne. A dermatologist can remove blackheads safely and prescribe special medications to help lessen or get rid of acne. These medicines are stronger and more effective than those sold over-the-counter in drugstores.

Ironically, although acne is generally more of a problem for boys than for girls, boys are often more reluctant to ask their parents to take them to a dermatologist. And even if the boy is willing, his parents may not think it is necessary. That's probably because, in our culture, it's more acceptable for girls to be concerned about their appearance. In contrast, people are more likely to expect boys to be able to ignore the problem and not let it bother them.

But that attitude makes no sense! As any boy with acne will tell you, it bothers him. If you have acne that makes you unhappy and affects the way you feel about yourself, explain this to your parents. Once they know how important the problem is, they'll be likely to want to help you do something about it.

Perspiration

Like oil glands, sweat glands become more active during puberty. Not only do boys who have entered puberty perspire more than they did as children, but their perspiration begins to have an adult odor. As a result, many boys become concerned that they have unpleasant body odor. Under most circumstances, just bathing daily and wearing clean clothes are enough to keep perspiration odor in check. But if you wish, you can use an underarm deodorant or antiperspirant to deal with perspiration odor. A deodorant eliminates odors; an antiperspirant also stops perspiration.

You may also notice that the skin around your genitals feels more moist or has a slightly different smell than when you were younger. That's because sweat and oil glands in this area have become more active too. Washing your genitals when you bathe and wearing clean underwear are enough to take care of any odor problems here as well.

Voice Changes

During puberty the vocal cords get longer and thicker, causing your voice to become lower and deeper. Often, the changes in a boy's voice are so gradual that they aren't really noticeable until his voice has become much lower. At other times, the drop in voice occurs more quickly.

Sometimes, in the process of growing to their adult size, the vocal cords can produce some pretty embarrassing sounds. You may find your voice suddenly "cracking," or becoming high and squeaky, out of nowhere. As luck would have it, this often seems to happen just when you really want to sound cool. Fortunately, the problem is temporary. As soon as your vocal cords are fully developed, the cracking will disappear.

You can also see for yourself that your vocal cords are growing. As they get larger, they push the Adam's apple out, making it more noticeable.

When Will You Start Puberty?

It's interesting to know when most boys begin puberty and when most will have completely matured. But you're likely to want to know when these things will happen to *you*. Although no one can answer that question simply by knowing your age, doctors do have a way of telling whether you have entered puberty and if so, how far along in this process you are. They use a series of spoon-shaped cups to measure your testicles. These cups are called an orchidometer. (*Orchido* comes from the Greek word meaning "testicle.")

The oval shapes on page 31 are flat, whereas an orchidometer is three-dimensional. But you can get a rough idea of whether you've started puberty by seeing which of the drawings is closest in size to one of your testicles. If your testicle is the size of one of the first three ovals, you haven't started puberty yet. However, if your testicle has reached the size of the fourth oval, you've started to develop sexually.

Most boys notice that their penis starts to grow when their testicles are somewhere between the sixth and the ninth oval in size. But, again, there are no hard-and-fast rules about this. Fully mature young men have testicles the size of the ninth oval or larger. If you have reached this point, you are either sexually mature or almost there.

By the way, this is a very good time to get in the habit of doing a monthly self-examination of your testicles. Although cancer of the testicles is very rare, it occurs most often in men between twenty

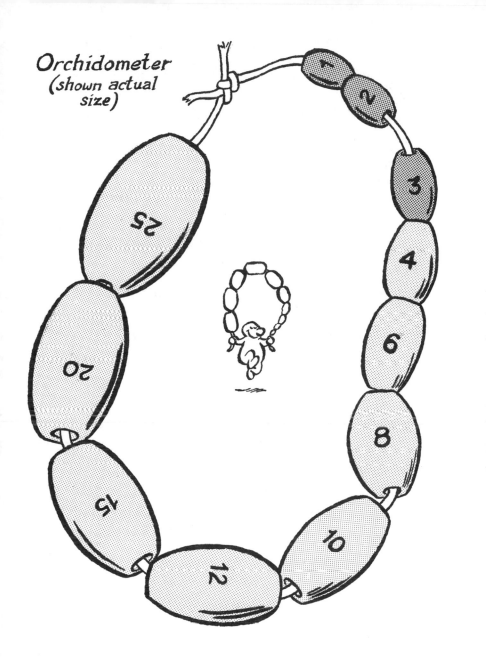

Orchidometer
(shown actual size)

and thirty-five years old and can develop in teenage boys as well. Fortunately, if caught early enough, it can be completely cured. That's why it's important to take a few minutes each month to check yourself out.

Testicular self-examination is very easy to do. Just roll your testicles between your thumb and first three fingers until you've felt the complete surface of each. Your testicles should feel egg-shaped, with a smooth surface. Be on the lookout for any lumps or unevenness in the shape or surface of the testicle, any places that seem firmer or thicker than the rest of the testicle, and any pain, dragging, or heavy sensations. Remember, you're examining only your testicles—not the scrotum or anything else. It's a good idea, though, to locate the epididymis (it's at the back of the testicle) and learn what it feels like. That way you won't confuse it with a lump.

It's easiest to do testicular examinations in the bathtub or shower, when the warm water helps to relax the scrotum. Exams should be done at least once a month. Picking a particular day, like the first of the month or the first Sunday, can help you remember to do it regularly.

When Will You Finish?

Unfortunately, not even
an orchidometer can
tell you how fast
you will mature.
It may take some
boys six years to
go through pu-
berty; others whip through
the whole process in a year.
Remember, whether you start
earlier or later than your friends
has nothing to do with how
rapidly you will move from one
stage to the next.

Most guys hope they go through puberty at
about the same time as their friends. That's because everyone is a little nervous about whether
things are going the way they're supposed to—and
being like other people helps reassure you that
you're normal. But each boy matures in his own
individual way, and being sooner or later, faster
or slower than others doesn't mean that some-

thing is wrong with you. And it certainly doesn't say anything about how much of a man or what kind of a man you will be when you grow up—that has to do with much more important things than your body.

Not So Sure You Like All These Changes?

Join the crowd. Most of us aren't completely comfortable with change, even when it's something we really want. Change is especially difficult when we don't have much control over when or how it happens. And this is particularly true when what's changing is your own body.

It can be hard when things change before you feel ready for them to change—or after you've felt ready for ages! And that's assuming the change is something you want. But as we've discussed, some of the changes that come with puberty—like getting pimples, having your voice crack, or developing swollen, sore breasts—aren't that great. Also, even good changes often have a downside. For example, you may enjoy the feeling that you are growing up and becoming a man, but not the fact that you have to do additional chores because "you're not a kid anymore."

So if you're not sure how you feel about all these changes—or if you feel good about them one day and unhappy the next—you're not alone. Change takes some getting used to, so be patient. After a while, you'll probably decide it was worth it. In the meantime, knowing what to expect and how to deal with things can help a lot.

CHAPTER 3

What's Going on Down There?

As many of you may already be aware, there are other things happening with your penis in addition to the changes discussed in chapter 2. Be-

sides growing larger and changing in appearance, a boy's penis also begins to feel and behave differently.

For example, at times your penis may get stiff or hard and jut out from your body. This is called an erection. It's perfectly normal; although if it happens when you don't want it to, it can be embarrassing.

The other event you may have experienced is ejaculation. Ejaculation occurs when a milky substance spurts from your penis. That milky substance is called semen, and it's made up of sperm and fluids produced by your body.

Both these changes can be upsetting if you don't know what's happening. So let's talk about how and why erections and ejaculations occur.

Erections

Your penis is the part of your body that allows you to place sperm into a woman's body. As we'll discuss in chapter 5, a man does this by putting his penis into a woman's vagina, a place between her legs that leads to her reproductive organs. However, it would be very difficult to do this if the penis remained soft. That's why a male's penis becomes hard, or erect, when he becomes sexually stimulated.

Throughout your body, including your penis, blood continually flows back and forth, bringing oxygen and nutrients that cells need to survive and function. When a man or a boy gets an erection, the blood flow to his penis increases. At the same time, the muscles at the base of the penis tighten temporarily so that the blood cannot flow back out. This makes the penis swell and stick out from the body.

When erect, the average adult male's penis is about six and a half inches long. Penises that are smaller when soft tend to add more in length than larger penises. So most men's penises are about the same length when erect. Penises also get thicker, as well as longer, when they become erect.

Young boys and even babies can have erections. However, since sexual stimulation is the most common cause of erections, they are much more likely to happen when you enter puberty.

Men and boys can be sexually stimulated by

many different things. Stroking or rubbing your penis, looking at a girl's breasts, or imagining yourself kissing or being naked with someone you find attractive are all examples of things that can cause erections.

It would be great if erections happened only when you wanted them. But they often occur when they are most unwelcome. Some boys develop an erection when they are in situations that make them nervous —such as giving a report in front of their class. At other times, it can happen when you are talking to a girl you like. It's also very common to wake up with an erection in the morning or to get an erection when you have to urinate.

And some erections seem to just spring up out of the blue, for no particular reason.

Erections last for anywhere from a few seconds to half an hour. Gradually, the muscles around the base of the penis begin to relax and blood flows back out again. The penis becomes soft and returns to its original size. This can happen all by itself. But it also happens after a male ejaculates.

Ejaculation

Ejaculation occurs when sperm are released from your penis. Since this can happen only after a boy has begun to produce sperm, many people consider a boy's first ejaculation to be a sign that he has become a man. Most boys have their first ejaculation when they are around thirteen or fourteen. However, some boys may be younger and some older.

Before sperm leave your penis, they've already traveled a long way. As you know from chapter 1, sperm begin in the testicles where they are manufactured, move up to the epididymis where they mature, and then are pushed through the vas deferens to the ampulla where they are stored.

When you become sexually stimulated, hormones signal your genitals to get ready to release this stored sperm. The seminal vesicles send a milky white fluid called semen into the ampulla. Semen mixes with sperm, giving the sluggish sperm a much-needed sugar boost. This sugar boost transforms the sperm into vigorous little swimmers with the energy needed to make the long trip ahead.

The prostate gland also adds fluid to the mixture of sperm and semen. Muscles around the prostate gland and in the penis then begin to contract, forcing the mixture out of the ampulla and down the urethra. These contractions cause the sperm to squirt out of the tip of the penis in a series of three or four spurts. Only a teaspoon or so of semen is ejaculated, but that small amount contains several hundred million sperm.

All this talk about spurting and contractions may not sound very appealing, but in fact the feelings a male has during ejaculation are extremely pleasurable. These feelings are called an orgasm, and orgasms are a big reason why having sex is such a popular activity.

Orgasms

Describing the feeling of an orgasm is very hard. That's partly because it's a little different for everybody and partly because the feelings can vary from time to time.

But mainly it's hard to describe because we just don't have the right words to do it justice. If you ask men to describe what an orgasm feels like, they'll probably say that it's fabulous, exciting, wonderful, or even the best thing ever.

AN ORGASM FEELS LIKE... LIKE... UM...

However, this doesn't really tell you much, except that they obviously enjoy it. Although women don't ejaculate, they have orgasms too. But they usually aren't any more successful than men in explaining why orgasms are so great.

It is possible to have the muscle contractions and sensations of orgasm before you are old enough to ejaculate. If so, you've probably discovered that these feelings result from stroking your penis. Or you may have already experienced both ejaculation and orgasm. If you've had an orgasm, what words would you choose to describe the feeling?

We+ Dreams

If you're like many boys, your first ejaculation may happen when you are asleep. Boys who aren't prepared for this often think they have wet the bed or have something wrong with them. They may be so embarrassed that they don't mention what has happened to anyone. Thus it can take them a while before they discover that nighttime ejaculations are normal.

When a male ejaculates in his sleep, the ejaculation is called a wet dream—*wet* because semen is a wet, sticky fluid, and *dream* because the boy or man is often having a sexy dream when he ejaculates, even if he doesn't remember it. But not all wet dreams are connected with actual dreams. Sometimes, they occur simply because the ampulla has become filled and needs to make room for new sperm being produced.

Even boys who are aware of what wet dreams are and why they occur may find them upsetting. Some worry that their parents, particularly their mother, will discover the evidence of ejaculation on their sheets. Wet dreams can also be distressing because they

are events that aren't under a boy's control. Thus guys often fear that, like spontaneous erections, a wet dream may happen when they are talking to an attractive girl or watching someone sexy on TV—in other words, in front of other people.

Fortunately, wet dreams happen only when you are asleep. Although you don't have control over ejaculations then, you do when you are awake. Unless you are stroking your penis, kissing someone you are attracted to, having sex, or purposefully doing something else that is sexually stimulating, you won't accidentally ejaculate while you're awake.

Masturbation

Stroking or rubbing the genitals for pleasure is called masturbation. Many people masturbate, including children, teenagers, married and unmarried adults, and elderly folks. They all do it for one reason: It feels good.

Most people today view masturbation as a normal and natural activity. But this has not always been the case. Years ago, it was often thought that masturbation was physically harmful and/or morally wrong. Some people's religious beliefs still lead them to conclude that masturbation is morally wrong. But it *definitely* is not physically harmful.

For example, masturbation will *not* give you pimples, cause you to go blind or insane, make hair grow on the palms of your hands, or result in warts—as many people believed in the past.

Nor will masturbating make you run out of sperm, as boys often fear. That would be impossible, since your body produces 100 million to 300 million sperm *each day.*

Finally, masturbating will not somehow "ruin you" for normal sexual relations. The idea behind this concern is that you may come to prefer masturbating to having sex with other people. But masturbation and sexual intercourse are two different activities. Having sex with another person involves close emotional feelings that masturbation doesn't. And you're not likely to want to miss this very nice emotional experience.

In fact, masturbation probably helps prepare

you for sex with another person. By exploring your own body, you have a chance to learn what feels best to you. Later, you'll be in a better position to let your sexual partner know the things that you like.

CHAPTER 4

Girls Are Changing Too

A quick look at girls your age will tell you that they are changing too. In fact, it's kind of hard not to notice some of these changes because they are so obvious.

Changes You Can See

The first sign of puberty in girls is that many begin to shoot up in height, well before any indication of the growth spurt in boys their

age. This explains why sixth- and seventh-grade girls are generally taller than boys in their class.

The other very noticeable change is that girls begin to develop breasts. Sometime between the ages of eight and sixteen, a girl's breasts begin to swell and grow out from her chest. This is a sign that her breasts are developing the milk glands that will make it possible for her to nurse a baby. Fat grows around these milk glands to protect them, giving breasts their adult shape.

A girl's hips and thighs also become wider and more curvy, but it's her new breasts that get most of the attention. And that has its advantages and disadvantages. Many girls are proud that their breasts announce to others that they are becoming women. On the other hand, sometimes it can seem that everyone is staring at their chests, and that often makes girls feel very self-conscious.

Just as some boys are concerned that their penises are too small, many girls worry whether their breasts are too little or too large. Moreover, breasts, like testicles, don't always grow at the same rate. Unless they know this is normal, girls can think that something is wrong with one breast or the other, or that they will end up with uneven breasts that make them look lopsided. They're usually relieved to know that, over time, the smaller breast will catch up.

Like boys, girls also begin to develop pubic hair and hair under their arms. The hair on their legs and sometimes their arms also becomes darker and thicker. Girls do not develop hair on their shoulders, back, or chest. However, some may find a few dark hairs appearing on their upper lip or growing in a fine line from their pubic hair to their belly button.

Because our culture tends to view women with less body hair as more feminine, many girls begin to shave their legs and underarms at this time. If they are bothered by hair on their upper lip, they may use beauty products to bleach these hairs so they are less noticeable. However, this is a matter of taste only. The amount of hair on a girl's body says nothing about how feminine she is.

In girls as well as boys, the activity of oil and sweat glands increases with puberty. This means that girls have the same concerns as you do about pimples and body odor.

WHAT'S GOING ON DOWN THERE?

Changes You Can't See

The changes in girls that you are probably most curious about are those you can't see—what's happening with their genitals, for example. Even boys who have helped bathe or dress their baby sisters usually find a girl's genitals to be a mystery. It might surprise you to know that they are a mystery to many girls as well.

The reason for that is simple. Most of a girl's sexual organs are inside her body. And even those on the outside aren't very visible. Since a girl's external genitals are flat against her body and farther back between her legs, the only way she can see them is by using a mirror. Until recently, girls were not encouraged to place a mirror between their legs so they could see what their genitals looked like; it's just wasn't consid-

ered ladylike. But now we realize that girls *should* learn everything they can about their own bodies. So a lot of girls are taking a look.

A Girl's External Genitals

If a girl places a mirror between her legs, she'll see something like the drawing below. At the top, near her abdomen, is where her first pubic hairs begin to appear. Farther down are two folds, or flaps, of skin, one on each side of a narrow separation. These are called the outer lips. Pubic

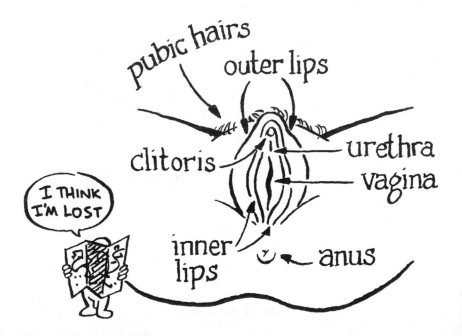

hair may have started to grow here as well. With puberty, the outer lips become darker and sort of wrinkled.

Inside the outer lips are another set of lips, called the inner lips. As a girl enters puberty, the inner lips begin to grow rapidly, becoming darker and more wrinkled. In many adult women the inner lips actually grow bigger than the outer lips and stick out from between the outer lips. In some ways, a woman's inner lips are very similar in appearance to the skin on your scrotum.

The inner lips protect three very important organs. At the bottom is the opening to the vagina. The vagina is the way in and out of a female's internal genital organs. Just above the vagina is the urethra, the opening through which a girl urinates. You'll notice that in females, the urethra and the sexual organs are completely separate, while in males, the vas deferens and the urethra are connected. Right above the urethra is the clitoris. Unlike the vagina and the urethra, the clitoris is not an opening. Instead, it's a little buttonlike bulge that is responsible for many of the pleasurable feelings women experience when they have sex.

A Girl's Internal Genitals

The internal female sexual organs are the ovaries, fallopian tubes, uterus, cervix, and vagina.

The ovaries are two egg-shaped organs on either side of a girl's abdomen. Their shape is very appropriate, because the ovaries contain the eggs. As you remember, a woman's eggs carry her half of the instructions for creating a baby. Al-

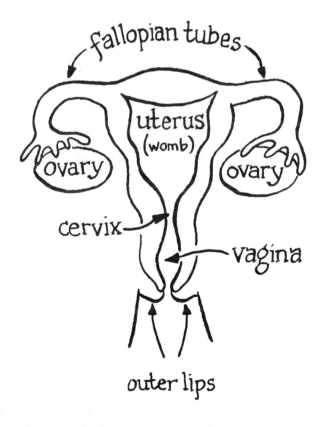

fallopian tubes

uterus (womb)

ovary

ovary

cervix

vagina

outer lips

though boys don't start making sperm until they enter puberty, girls are born with all of their eggs. However, the eggs don't start maturing until puberty.

An egg must travel all the way from the ovary to the uterus, where a baby develops, if a child is to be born. This is where the fallopian tubes come in. They provide an avenue from the ovary to the uterus.

The uterus is the large triangular organ between the fallopian tubes. The uterus is also called the womb, and it's the place where a baby spends the nine months before it is born, growing and developing.

At the bottom of the uterus is the cervix, a knob of flesh with a small hole in the center. One purpose of the cervix is to help keep germs from entering the uterus. The cervix also helps contain the baby inside the uterus. When the baby is ready to be born, the hole in the middle of the cervix widens so that the baby can leave the uterus and enter the vagina.

The vagina is the passageway into and out of a woman's reproductive organs. By putting his penis into a woman's vagina, a man can place sperm in her body. The vagina is also the way a baby gets out of its mother's body. The walls of the vagina are very elastic and can stretch wide enough to make room for a penis and even for a baby.

Menstruation

Just as ejaculation is considered a sign that a boy is able to reproduce, something happens in a girl's life that lets her know that she has become able to have a baby. That event is called menstruation.

Sometime between the ages of eleven and fourteen, give or take a year or two, a girl's eggs begin to mature. Once a month, a single egg ripens and is released from an ovary. The fringe-like "fingers" at the end of the fallopian tube sweep the egg toward the entrance to the tube. As it travels down the fallopian tube, the egg may meet and unite with a sperm. The joining of an egg and a sperm is called fertilization, and only a fertilized egg can grow into a baby.

Meanwhile, the uterus has been getting ready for the egg, just in case it has been fertilized. The lining of the uterus has developed a thick spongy

cushion of blood-filled tissue to provide a fertilized egg with the food and support it will need to grow into a baby. For a number of reasons, most of the time the egg reaches the uterus without having been fertilized. Unlike a fertilized egg, an unfertilized egg does not attach to the lining of the uterus. Instead, it simply disintegrates and disappears.

Without a fertilized egg to nourish, there is no need for the thick lining of the uterus. It begins to shed slowly, dribbling out of the vagina for the next two to seven days. The time when a young woman is bleeding is called a menstrual period, menstruation, or just a period, for short.

This menstrual cycle occurs every month from a girl's first period until she reaches her forties or fifties. Then her ovaries begin to produce ripe eggs less frequently, until they stop altogether. At that point, a woman is no longer able to have children.

Does It Hurt?

Boys often wonder if it hurts when a girl bleeds during menstruation. The answer is sometimes, but not in the way you may imagine. Menstruation is not like having a cut. The pain we feel when we are cut is our body's way of alerting us to the fact that we've been wounded and should do something to take care of the injury. But menstruation is not a wound. It's a natural part of a woman's life. So there's no need for the body to signal to girls that something is wrong.

However, menstruation can sometimes be uncomfortable. Many girls and women get an occasional cramping feeling in their abdomen during their period. Some girls have cramps only rarely, whereas others have cramps every month. Usually, cramps are mild and last only for a day, but a few girls and women have severe cramps that last longer and make them miserable.

How Much Does a Girl Bleed?
Does She Have to Wear a Bandage?

The amount a girl or woman bleeds varies from person to person. Some girls lose a couple of spoonfuls of blood each month; others lose a cup's worth. In any event, it's enough blood that a girl needs to wear something to keep it from staining her clothes. Some girls wear an absorbent cotton pad that fits on top of the crotch of their under-

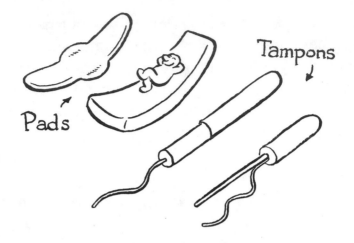

Pads

Tampons

pants, and others use a tampon. A tampon is also made of absorbent cotton, but it is shaped like a lipstick tube so that it can fit inside the vagina. A tampon is inserted with an applicator or the finger and is pulled out by a string attached to the bottom. Since a woman's vagina can stretch to fit a penis or a baby, there's plenty of room in there for a tampon to fit comfortably.

What Makes Some Girls So Cranky When They're Having Their Period?

A female's body undergoes many hormonal changes in the days right before her period and for the first day or two of her period. These hormonal fluctuations can cause her breasts to become swollen and tender and her body to feel bloated. Hormonal ups and downs can also make some girls feel more emotional than usual. They may be sad, irritable, or more easily upset than they are ordinarily. These physical and emotional symptoms are called the premenstrual syndrome, or PMS. Some females rarely experience PMS or have only mild symptoms, but others are bothered by PMS almost every month. Fortunately, the symptoms of PMS last for only a few days. And as a girl gets more experience with having her period, she usually becomes better at handling the emotional swings.

CHAPTER 5

Having Sex

Since having sex is a topic that many boys are *very* interested in, some of you may have turned to this chapter right off the bat. You're welcome to read the chapters of this book in any order. But if you start here, be sure to go back later and read chapters 1 to 4. A lot of the words used in chapter 5 are explained in these chapters, so they may help clear up any questions that you have.

Being Sexual

Strictly speaking, when we say that a man and a woman—or a boy and a girl—are having sex, we mean that the man is putting his penis into the w̲ ̲ ̲an's vagina. But if that were all there was to it, this chapter would be very short.

It's important to know that putting a penis into a vagina is only one part of being sexual with another person. Kissing a girl that you are attracted to, hugging her, or touching, stroking, or caressing her body—and having her do these things to you—are all ways of being sexual that don't involve actually having sex.

Both boys and girls find being sexual with another person is very enjoyable. In addition to feeling great physically, it usually makes the two people feel emotionally close to each other. For many people, this emotional closeness can be the best part of being sexual with one another.

Having Sex

Most of the time, having sex begins with two people just touching each other—kissing, holding, stroking, and caressing each other's faces and bodies. These things are very pleasurable by themselves. But they also help prepare the couple's bodies for having sex. Because of this, these activities are called foreplay.

Kissing and touching a woman's body in this way causes a man to have an erection, which helps him insert his penis in the woman's vagina. A woman's body responds to kissing and a man's touch as well. Her vagina begins to produce a slippery fluid that makes it easier for the man to slide his penis into her. But these changes are only *in preparation* for having sex. They don't mean that a man or a woman *has* to have sex. In fact, many times, the couple decides not to go any farther. They may feel that they are too young to have sex, that they don't know each other well enough or want to wait until they are married to have sex, or they may not have access to birth control and don't want to have unprotected sex.

If the couple does decide to have sex, the man puts his penis into the woman's vagina. Even though the man's penis is much bigger when it's erect, the vagina is very elastic. So it can easily expand to make room for the penis.

As the man and woman move their bodies together, the penis slides back and forth in the
woman's vagina. This
stimulates the nerves
at the end of the
penis and
in the vagina
and clitoris.
These feel-
ings are
a lot like
the physical
sensations that come from being sexual with
someone in other ways. However, they are generally more intense and usually result in an
orgasm.

Although the thought of having sex is attractive to a lot of boys, some of you may be thinking
instead that all this sounds messy, awkward, and
kind of unappealing. If so, you're partly right.
Ejaculations and vaginal fluids are wet and occasionally messy. And sometimes people do feel
clumsy when they are trying to get their bodies to
work together. But when two people know each
other well, trust each other, and feel ready to have

sex, the messy and awkward part doesn't matter very much. That's because the physical pleasure and emotional closeness that can be part of having sex are well worth the bother.

Being Sure You Are Ready

Having sex can be a very intense experience—and one that may lead to things you might not have anticipated. That's why it's a good idea not to have sex until you are ready. Of course, one thing that can result from having sex is a baby. We'll talk more about that in chapter 6. But there can be other consequences as well. For example, since having sex can make people feel closer to each other, it may hurt more if you are dumped by a girl you've been having sex with.

Unfortunately, it's not always easy to know if you are ready. Both boys and girls are often under a lot of pressure to have sex. This can make it very hard for you to tell whether you are ready to have sex or just feel it's something you *should* do.

These pressures can take a lot of forms. Some kids think that having sex will make them popular or prove that they are well liked. Others may feel pressured to have sex so that their friends will quit teasing them or to prove to themselves that they are normal. Both boys and girls may think that having sex with someone they are interested in will tie that person to them. (This *never* works,

by the way.) Others feel pressured to have sex to show that they love someone.

Finally, sometimes the pressure of feeling different—like being the only kid you know who isn't having sex—is the worst pressure of all. But before you decide that you're the last virgin in town, keep in mind that not every boy who says he is having sex is telling the truth. Often, people claim to be doing more than they really are in an effort to seem cool.

Handling pressures that other people place on you, as well as the ones you place on yourself, is often very difficult. But regardless of what others are doing, remember: You don't have to be sexual or have sex with anyone until *you* feel ready! Doing something you don't feel ready to do usually turns out not to be much fun and can leave you feeling worse instead of better. This is especially true when it comes to having sex.

Pressuring Others

Just as you have every right to say no to others when they pressure you, you need to respect other people's wishes as well. For example, it is a very bad idea to try to pressure a girl into having sex with you if she doesn't want to. At a bare minimum, it will probably make her feel uncomfortable or unhappy—and you certainly don't want to do that to someone you care about. It may also cause her to dislike you or not want to be around you. Worse, depending on the kind of pressure you use, it can get you into serious legal trouble.

Using physical force to pressure a person to have sex is called rape. Rape is a crime that is punishable by a prison term. But there are other kinds of pressure that may be considered rape as well. Depending on your state laws and the situation, driving a girl out to a deserted area at night and then threatening to leave her there unless she has sex with you may legally be rape too.

Also, remember that—when it comes to having sex—people always have the right to change their minds. A girl may have agreed to have sex with you but then decide that she made a mistake. If she changes her mind and says no, you have to stop—even if you think she's being unfair. Of course, you have the right to change your mind as well. Just because you indicated that you wanted to have sex doesn't mean you're obligated to go through with it, no matter what the other person says. If it doesn't feel right to you, it's a good idea not to do it.

Homosexuality

Most sexual couples consist of a male and a female. These people are called heterosexuals because they are sexually attracted to individuals of the opposite sex. (*Hetero* means "other.") But this is not the only way that human beings can be sexual. Some people are sexually attracted to others of their own sex. These people are called homosexuals. (*Homo* means "same.") You may also hear ho-

mosexuals referred to as gay. Still other individuals are bisexual, or attracted to both males and females. (*Bi* means "two.")

Homosexuals (and bisexuals, for that matter) can be men or women, old or young, and from any race or ethnic group. Unlike the stereotypes you may have seen, they usually look like everyone else in the population and have the same jobs and interests as other people.

Many homosexuals have had sexual partners of the opposite sex at some time in their lives. They may even have been married and had children. This is because they may not have realized that they were gay until they became attracted to someone of the same sex. Or they may have known they were homosexual but tried very hard to live the way society in general says people should live—as heterosexuals.

Homosexuals are sexual with each other in most of the same ways as heterosexuals are. They enjoy kissing each other and touching, caressing, and stroking each other's bodies. And they experience orgasms just as everyone else does. The biggest difference is that for homosexuals, having sex does not involve putting a penis into a vagina.

Many young people wonder what "makes" a person gay. At this point, it's unclear why some people grow up to become homosexuals while others are heterosexuals. Recent research suggests that some people may be born with a tendency to become gay. But this is probably not the case for all homosexuals.

One thing that is certain is that homosexuals don't *choose* to be gay. People generally don't have much control over the type of individuals they are sexually attracted to. They only have control over whether they act on their feelings. Given the prejudice and discrimination gay people still face, most would never have chosen to be homosexual if they had felt there were another alternative.

You may have heard some very negative things about homosexuals. Most often, these opinions are based on misinformation and fear. The fact is that a person's heterosexuality, homosexuality, or bisexuality has nothing to do with whether he or she is a good person. So it makes much more sense to judge people on important things—such as whether they are kind, helpful, honest, and caring—than on whether they are attracted to people of the same or opposite sex.

CHAPTER 6

Making (and Not Making) a Baby

By now, you know that a baby is formed when a man's sperm unites with a woman's egg. And you know how sperm get inside a woman. But you are probably wondering exactly how the sperm and the egg get together and what happens after that. The answer to these questions is determined by a couple of things.

The most important factor is whether a sperm and an egg actually have a chance to meet in the first place. As you may remember, a woman's ovaries release a mature egg only once a month. If a couple has sex when there is no mature egg available, fertilization can't occur. Nor can anything happen if the egg is released but there are no sperm around.

But the story can be very different if a couple has sex around the time when the woman is ovulating, or releasing an egg. Upon being released, the egg is swept into the nearest fallopian tube. Meanwhile, the sperm are busy making the long trip up the vagina, past the cervix, and into the uterus. From the uterus, the sperm begin to swim up both fallopian tubes.

Sperm that enter the empty tube will not encounter an egg. Only those that swim into the tube containing the egg will have a chance to fertilize it and begin a pregnancy. An egg can be fertilized by only one sperm, however. As soon as a sperm breaks into the egg cell, no other sperm can get in. Thus, of the millions of sperm that started out, rel-

atively few manage to reach the egg, and only one actually unites with it. If you think about it, that's like winning the world's largest marathon race.

The fertilized egg cell travels down the fallopian tube, dividing again and again until it consists of many cells. After about five days, it reaches the uterus, where it plants itself in the thick, nourishing lining. Within the protective uterus, it grows and develops over the next nine months into a baby.

At the end of this time, the baby is able to live outside the uterus and is ready to be born. The mother's cervix widens, and her uterus begins to contract over and over again. These muscle contractions slowly push the baby out of the uterus, through the cervix, and into the vagina. The walls of the vagina stretch wide so that the baby can pass through. In most cases, the first part of the baby to come out of the vagina is the head, followed by the rest  of its body. But some babies are born feet first. When this happens, it is called a breech birth.

Boys often ask if this is painful for the mother. Although some women find childbirth to be extremely painful, others find it much less so. It's also possible for a particular woman to have a difficult time with the birth of one child and an easier time with another.

Twins

Usually, a woman gives birth to one child at a time. Occasionally, however, her ovaries may release two eggs at the same time. If both eggs become fertilized, twins—or two babies—can result, one from each egg. Twins that develop from two different eggs are called fraternal twins. Fraternal twins can be the same sex or different sexes. They may look a lot like or not much like each other at all. In fact, they are just like any two brothers, two sisters, or a brother and a sister—except that they were born at the same time.

Twins can occur in another way as well. In this case, a fertilized egg splits completely in half, forming two separate babies. Since they started out from the same fertilized egg, these twins are

2 EGGS, 2 SPERM   FRATERNAL TWINS

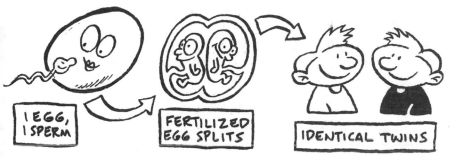

1 EGG, 1 SPERM   FERTILIZED EGG SPLITS   IDENTICAL TWINS

identical. Not only do they look alike, but they are both the same sex.

Births of more than two babies at the same time are much rarer, but they do occur. Recently, a woman gave birth to seven infants at once. Multiple births are more likely to happen when a woman has been taking fertility drugs.

Being Careful Not to Make a Baby

Many people may want to have sex but do not wish to make, or conceive, a baby. If so, there are several things they can do to prevent the conception of a baby. Most of these things are designed to keep mature eggs from being released or to prevent sperm and eggs from coming in contact with each other. Because these methods are used to prevent conception, they are called contraceptives, contraceptive methods, or birth control. Some forms of birth control are much more effective than others.

The Rhythm Method

Since a woman releases a mature egg only once a month, if a couple is careful not to have sex around that time, a pregnancy shouldn't result. This strategy is called the rhythm method. While the rhythm method looks good on paper, there are some definite problems with using it in real life.

The biggest difficulty is determining when an egg is actually going to be released. A woman ovu-

lates halfway through her menstrual cycle. But since the length of her cycle can vary from month to month, predicting when the middle will occur is pretty risky. In addition, the egg can be fertilized up to three or four days after it is released. This means that even if a couple can determine the day of ovulation, having sex on that day and for the next few days might still result in pregnancy.

To make matters even more complicated, sperm can live for three to five days inside the woman. Thus, if a couple wants to avoid making a baby, they should not have sex for up to five days before the woman ovulates because there may still be sperm around when the egg is released. Therefore, assuming the couple can accurately predict when the woman is going to ovulate (and that is a *giant* if), they must avoid having sex on the day of ovulation and for five days before and four days afterward if they don't want to conceive a baby. Altogether, that means a total of ten days out of every twenty-eight-day cycle. As you can guess, this method doesn't work very well.

Withdrawal

A man may also try to avoid a pregnancy by withdrawing his penis from the woman's vagina before he ejaculates. The idea behind this strategy is to keep sperm from being placed inside the woman. Unfortunately, there are a lot of problems with this contraceptive method as well.

First, when a man or a boy is excited, he may not withdraw his penis in time—and even a small amount of sperm can make the woman pregnant. Second, even before ejaculation, a few drops of fluid appear at the tip of the penis. This fluid may contain sperm that could impregnate the woman. Finally, ejaculating near the opening of the woman's vagina may also result in pregnancy. In this case, the sperm may swim into the opening and enter the woman's vagina.

Birth Control Pills, Norplant, and Depo-Provera

Birth control pills are hormone pills that keep a girl's or a woman's ovaries from releasing mature eggs. This is a very effective form of birth control *if* the woman takes the pills every day according to schedule, regardless of whether she intends to have sex. In addition to being a method of contraception, birth control pills are sometimes prescribed to help get a girl's irregular or abnormally long menstrual periods back on track.

Norplant and Depo-Provera are also hormones that prevent the release of mature eggs, but they are not given in pill form. With Norplant, the hormones are contained in little tubes that are placed just under the skin of a woman's or girl's arm. These tubes slowly release the hormones over a period of years. Depo-Provera is

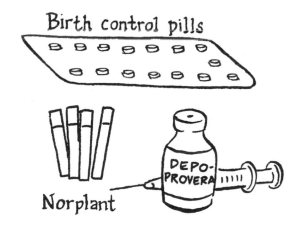

Birth control pills

Norplant

DEPO-PROVERA

given by injection every three months. The advantage of these two methods is that a girl does not have to remember to take a daily pill.

Diaphragms and Cervical Caps

Diaphragms and cervical caps block the entrance to the uterus, so that sperm cannot enter. Both are round latex shields that a woman places against her cervix before she has sex. The 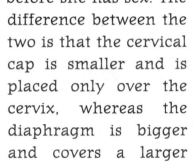 difference between the two is that the cervical cap is smaller and is placed only over the cervix, whereas the diaphragm is bigger and covers a larger area. A woman puts the diaphragm or cap in each time she has sex. Diaphragms and caps should be used with a spermicide—a jelly, cream, or foam containing chemicals that kill sperm—to be effective.

IUDs

An IUD, or intrauterine device, is a thin plastic or copper device that is placed inside the uterus. This device works differently from most forms of birth control. Instead of preventing fertilization, it keeps the fertilized egg from planting itself in the lining of the uterus. An IUD must be inserted by a doctor, where it remains for a period of a few years or until the woman wishes to become pregnant. Because IUDs have been linked to infection, they are no longer manufactured in the United States.

Condoms

Condoms are made of latex and shaped like a long balloon. They fit over an erect penis like a very thin glove and catch the semen when a man ejaculates. Since semen can sometimes leak out, condoms are most effective when used with a spermicide. Most condoms on the market are for men. But there are condoms for women as well. These condoms are bigger and fit inside the vagina.

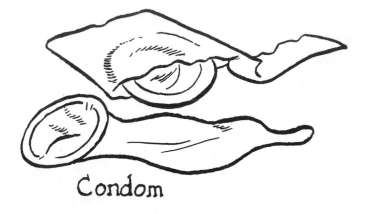

Condom

Putting on a male condom is very easy. The condom comes rolled up in a little packet. When your penis is erect, take the condom out of the package, place it at the tip of your penis, and roll the sides down the length of your penis. Be sure there is a space left at the tip of the condom to catch and hold semen.

Used correctly and every time a couple has sex, condoms are a very effective form of birth control. But they have a second, and equally important, use as well. Unlike other contraceptives, condoms can help prevent the spread of diseases, such as AIDS. (More about this in chapter 7.)

That's why a couple should always use a condom, even if they are also using another form of birth control.

Where to Get Birth Control

Some forms of contraception, such as condoms and spermicides, can be purchased at any drugstore and at some convenience stores and supermarkets.

Anyone can buy these contraceptives, regardless of his or her age.

Girls must go to a doctor to get birth control pills, Norplant, Depo-Provera, diaphragms, cervical caps, or IUDs. If you know a girl who is interested in obtaining one of these forms of birth control, she should discuss this with her parents. But if she is reluctant to talk to them, she can still get contraceptives on her own at Planned Parenthood or other family clinics. Visits to these clinics are confidential. That means the doctors and nurses will not notify your parents or anyone else that you have gone there for help.

Why Birth Control Fails

As you probably know, the number of pregnancies among teenagers has soared in recent years. Thus you don't have to be a rocket scientist to know that birth control sometimes fails. There can be many different reasons for this.

Probably the biggest reason for the "failure" of birth control is that the couple wasn't using it in the first place. Many young people in particular have mistaken ideas as to when a woman can get pregnant. They may think that a girl can't get pregnant the first time she has sex, or if she has sex during her period, or if she has sex standing up—so they don't use contraceptives under these circumstances. But girls can and do get pregnant in all these situations.

Another reason why birth control may not work is that the method chosen—such as the rhythm method or withdrawal—isn't very effective. Or the method may be effective but the person had difficulty using it correctly. For example, a girl may forget to take her birth control pills consistently or may insert her diaphragm the wrong way. If used correctly, birth control pills, diaphragms, cervical caps, and condoms are very effective. Norplant, Depo-Provera, and IUDs are also very effective, and a woman doesn't have to worry if she is using them correctly.

Sometimes birth control doesn't work because a person secretly wants it to fail. Both boys and girls can feel pressured to have a baby. A boy may feel that by making a girl pregnant, he proves that he is a man. A girl may want to have a baby

so that she knows she always has someone to love her. A boy or a girl who is in love with someone may feel that having a baby with that person will help keep the couple together.

Unfortunately, when people are under these pressures, they may not always be honest about whether they are using birth control. Boys may promise to withdraw before ejaculating and then "accidentally" ejaculate too soon. Or a girl may say she is taking birth control pills when she is not. Boys and girls who are not honest about birth control aren't doing this to be mean or because they are bad people. They just think their lives will be happier somehow if they make a baby. That's why both a boy and a girl should *each* take responsibility for birth control. That way, each can be sure that precautions have truly been taken.

CHAPTER 7

Staying Healthy

There are many ways that disease-causing germs can be transmitted, or passed from one person to another. You're probably most familiar with those that are transmitted through the air. For example, when someone who has a cold or the flu sneezes or coughs, that person sends germs into the air. If you breathe in these germs, you can get sick too. Other illnesses are transmitted by germs in food or water.

Certain germs are transmitted through sexual activity. The diseases caused by these germs are called sexually transmitted diseases, or STDs. AIDS is the most serious STD, but there are many other STDs as well. Some of these STDs can also be very serious, but others are much less of a problem.

Learning about STDs and how to protect yourself from them is an important part of growing up.

You probably have a lot of questions about STDs, especially AIDS. Because there are some things about AIDS that make it different from other STDs, we'll discuss it last. First, let's look at some of the other serious STDs.

Syphilis, Gonorrhea, and Chlamydia

Syphilis, gonorrhea, and chlamydia are three common STDs that can all have serious long-term effects if not treated. Although these diseases are

Syphilis, Gonorrhea, and Chlamydia

usually passed from one person to another by having sex, they can be spread in other ways as well. Syphilis causes sores on the mouth or on the genitals. Putting your mouth in contact with these sores can result in your becoming infected as well. A pregnant woman who has syphilis, gonorrhea, or chlamydia can also pass the disease on to her baby before it is born or during birth.

Untreated syphilis can result in blindness, inability to walk, loss of bladder control, and even insanity and death. Babies infected with syphilis before birth may be born blind, mentally retarded, or with other serious birth defects. Gonorrhea can also cause blindness in untreated babies. Chlamydia is by far the most common STD and is a serious cause of infertility, or the inability to have children, particularly in women. One reason chlamydia is so widespread is that it has no symptoms, so people are usually unaware that they are infected. As a result, they do not get treatment and pass the disease on unknowingly.

Like chlamydia, untreated syphilis and gonorrhea can also result in infertility. Fortunately, there are drugs that can cure syphilis, gonorrhea, and chlamydia. But it's important to begin treatment as soon as possible, before the disease has had a chance to cause permanent damage.

Genital Herpes

There are many different types of herpes. Some, like chicken pox, are not sexually transmitted. Cold sores or fever blisters—blisterlike sores around the mouth, nose, and eyes—may be passed from one person to another through contact with an open sore. But genital herpes, a disease that results in painful sores in the genital area, is spread through sexual contact.

Genital herpes is different from syphilis, gonorrhea, and chlamydia in one important way. Unlike these diseases, there is no cure for genital herpes. Drugs can help make the sores go away, but the germs are never completely destroyed. Instead, the germs become quiet, or inactive. At some point in the future, they may resurface, becoming active again and causing new sores.

Genital herpes is very contagious. It is easily spread during sex through contact with infected sores, semen, or fluids from the vagina. Although herpes is usually spread when there are sores present, it can also be transmitted when an infected person has no symptoms.

Pregnant women who have active herpes are more likely to have miscarriages, premature births, and stillborn babies (babies who are dead at birth). Women with active herpes can also pass the disease on to their infants, either before or during birth. In newborn babies, herpes can result in blindness, brain damage, and death. Fortunately, treatment can reduce the length and seriousness of active disease and thus limit its ability to cause these problems.

Genital Warts

Genital warts are usually painless and are very similar to warts on the rest of the body. In men, they can occur on the penis, scrotum, and anus. Genital warts are spread when a person's genitals come in direct contact with a genital wart on someone else. Genital warts cannot spread to other parts of your body, however, nor can other types of warts spread to your genitals.

Genital warts are a concern because they can be involved in causing cancer of the cervix or vagina in women. Of course, you don't have a cervix or vagina, so you don't have to worry that you will develop these cancers. But you certainly wouldn't want to spread these warts to a girl who would be vulnerable.

"Kids Like Me Don't Get STDs"

It can be hard to imagine yourself or your friends getting an STD. But STDs can strike *anyone* who is having sex. It doesn't matter whether you are

I'M SAFE... ONLY PEOPLE LIKE HIM GET SEXUALLY TRANSMITTED DISEASES!

a boy or a girl, what race or religion you are, or whether you have just had sex once or have been having sex for years.

In fact, the biggest group of people with STDs are those between fifteen and twenty-four years of age. So you need to know the symptoms of STDs, where to get treatment, and how to protect yourself.

Warning Signs of STDs

There are a number of symptoms that *may* signal that you have an STD and should see a doctor:

WHAT'S GOING ON DOWN THERE?

sores, rashes, blisters, or warts on your genitals, anus, or mouth; pain or a burning feeling when you urinate; pain when you have sexual intercourse; swelling or itching around your genitals or anus; or an unusual discharge from your penis.

Often, guys who have one or more of these warning signs are very relieved when the symptoms disappear on their own. When this happens, it's easy to assume that whatever problem you may have had is gone. But STDs aren't like colds or the flu, which will eventually go away by themselves. The symptoms of an STD may disappear, but the disease usually can't be cured or controlled without medical treatment.

Going to the Doctor

Although it's extremely important to see a doctor if you have any of the symptoms of an STD, many boys panic at the thought. After all, it's never easy to say to your parents, "Hey, I think I have this gross disease that you can get from having sex. Will you take me to a doctor?" And for many kids, admitting to their parents that they are having sex may seem worse than having a serious disease.

If your parents already know that you've been having sex or if you and your parents have talked about sex or STDs before, you — should feel comfortable enough to go to them for help. Even if you think discussing your problem with them will be difficult, it's good to give it a try.

But if you can't do this, you can still get medical treatment. Most areas have Planned Parenthood or public health clinics that offer confidential treatment for STDs. Remember, this means that the clinic will treat you without notifying your parents. You can find these clinics by looking in your local phone book under Planned Parenthood or your city or county health department.

Preventing STDs

It's a lot easier to avoid getting an STD in the first place than to have to worry about whether you have one or how you're going to get treatment. There are several ways that you can reduce the chance that you will develop an STD. First, since these diseases are sexually transmitted, one way to prevent them is not to have sex. Of course, this doesn't mean forever! However, sometimes it's a good idea to postpone sex until you are a little older and more mature. As discussed in chapter 6, not everyone is emotionally ready to have sex when they're a young teenager. Avoiding an STD is an additional benefit of waiting a while longer.

But if you're having sex, using a condom is your best protection against disease. STDs result when your genitals come in contact with the infected sores, skin, vaginal fluids, or semen of someone else. If you wear a condom, your penis is protected from these sources of infection. And if you're the one who has an STD, a condom keeps your infection from coming in contact with someone else's genitals.

Finally, use your head. Don't have sex with someone if you notice that person has symptoms of an STD. Don't kiss someone on the mouth who has a sore there. And if you learn that someone whom you've had sex with has an STD, don't wait to see if you develop symptoms. Have yourself checked out anyway.

AIDS (Acquired Immune Deficiency Syndrome)

A combination of two things makes AIDS a special STD. First, there is no cure for AIDS, although there are drugs that can help control the germ that causes the disease. Second, while it may take years or even decades, almost everyone who has AIDS eventually dies from it.

AIDS is caused by a virus called the human immunodeficiency virus, or HIV for short. HIV at-

tacks the cells in the body that protect a person from disease. When these cells are destroyed, the body is unable to fight off infections and cancers.

Over time, one or more of these infections or cancers usually prove fatal.

A person whose body can no longer fight off serious illnesses because of HIV infection is said to have AIDS. However, it is possible to be infected with HIV for many years before the body's defense system begins to crumble. Until then, a person may seem healthy, with no symptoms to indicate that he or she is infected. Nevertheless, even without symptoms, an infected person can still pass HIV on to others.

HIV is transmitted through blood, semen, and vaginal fluids. Thus one way people can get HIV is by having sex with an infected person. But HIV can also be passed from one person to another by sharing needles to inject illegal drugs. This is because there may be blood left on the needle after a person has used it. And like many other STDs, HIV can be transmitted from a pregnant woman to her unborn baby. Several years ago, HIV could also be transmitted through a blood transfusion. But today, all blood used for transfusions in the United States is tested to make sure that it doesn't contain the virus.

HIV *cannot* be transmitted by normal everyday

contact with an infected person. That's because these germs can't survive in open air. This means that you cannot get HIV from hugging someone, using a public toilet, swimming in a pool or sitting in a hot tub with someone, drinking from his or her glass or sharing food, using the same telephone, or having someone sneeze on you, for example. Even kissing someone lightly will not result in your getting the disease. And you definitely can't get HIV from donating blood for a transfusion or receiving a shot from a nurse or a doctor.

Like other STDs, HIV does not discriminate. Anybody who has sex or shares needles with an infected person can get HIV—regardless of age, sex, or race, or whether you are heterosexual, homosexual, or bisexual.

Treating HIV Infection

Although researchers have not found a way to cure HIV, they have made a lot of progress in treating the disease. Recently, new drugs have become available that can eliminate most of the virus from an infected person's blood, at least for a while. Many people who have been taking these new drugs have become much healthier. This is great! But, unfortunately, the success of these drugs has led some people to feel that HIV isn't that big a problem anymore. "If I get infected," they think, "these new drugs will take care of it." However, it's very important to know that these drugs don't work for everyone. And the drugs may not work forever, even in people who do benefit.

Preventing HIV Infection

At present, there is no vaccine that can prevent HIV infection. However, some of the most important ways of preventing other STDs work equally well in preventing HIV infection. If you are not having sex or sharing needles to inject illegal drugs, you don't have to worry about getting HIV. If you are having sex, using a condom is a must! Not just some of the time, but all of the time.

Also, if you choose to get a tattoo, be sure you are careful. If the person giving you the tat-

USE ONLY BRAND-NEW, STERILIZED NEEDLES FOR TATTOOS

Be Safe

too uses a needle that has been used on someone else before you, the danger is the same as if you were sharing needles to inject drugs. So be sure the person uses a brand-new sterilized needle. You should also check to make sure that the equipment used to pierce ears and other parts of the body has been sterilized.

On the other hand, looking for symptoms in others before having sex with them isn't very useful. That's because it takes a long time for symptoms of HIV infection to appear in most people. This is especially true for young people who are infected, since they probably haven't been infected very long. Thus you are not likely to know whether someone else is infected or not. And kids your age who are infected often don't know it either. Since there is no way of telling who's infected, you need to use a condom every time you have sex with someone.

You should also know that doctors can now stop the transmission of HIV from a pregnant woman to her baby by giving the mother certain drugs during her pregnancy. Thus, pregnant women should be tested for HIV so doctors can prescribe these drugs if they are needed.

Getting Discouraged About Sex?

About this time, you may be feeling that having sex is a very dangerous activity that should be avoided at all costs. Or at the very least, it may seem as if there's so much to worry about that it couldn't be very enjoyable.

But that's certainly not the case. Sex is a perfectly natural and wonderful part of life. And having to take care of yourself doesn't spoil it. After all, you buckle your seat belt when getting in a car, wear a helmet when riding a motorcycle, and put on a life jacket when going out on a speed-boat—and none of these things takes the fun out of the ride.

CHAPTER 8

"Is This Normal?"

Most boys (and girls) going through puberty worry about being normal. With all the changes happening to them, many are afraid that something may go wrong. Since they don't know exactly what to expect, they spend a lot of time comparing themselves to other kids their age. They figure that if they are like everyone else, they must be OK.

The only problem with this is that "normal" and "like everyone else" are often not the same. When people say that a boy is normal, they mean that he's healthy and developing in the way that he should. In contrast, when boys use the expression "like everyone else," they don't really mean like *everyone* else, but like most of the guys they know or want to be like.

Sometimes, being like your friends can seem almost as important as being normal. But there's a big difference in reality! In a year or two, many of the things that make you feel different from your friends today, such as taking forever to reach your adult height, will no longer matter. And other things that you don't like now, such as the way your voice sounds, may be among the things you like best about yourself later.

In the meantime, it helps a lot to have someone older you can ask about things that concern you. Often, the best person is your dad. Ask him how he dealt with puberty. Believe it or not, he'll probably be flattered that you're interested in his experience and what he has to say. Older brothers, coaches, and even your friends' fathers can be good people to talk with as well.

But don't forget your mother. Many boys find that she knows a lot about a male's body and the changes a boy goes through, even if she is a woman. And your mom is a good source of information about what's going on with girls your age. After all, she was one once.

It may also help you to read about some of the things that other boys worry about:

"I'm getting weird-looking little bumps around my penis! How do I get rid of them?"

Many boys are upset by the appearance of bumps on the skin around the base of the penis. Although these bumps are often mis-taken for pimples, they are actually pubic hairs trying to break through the sur-face of the skin. As soon as these hairs push through the skin, the bumps disappear. Other small bumps on the skin of the penis and the scrotum are newly active sweat and oil glands. They are responsible for the fact that the skin on your genitals has become more moist.

"The doctor said I'm probably going to be on the short side. He says I'm normal, but if that's true, then how come my dad is so upset? Is there anything that can make me taller?"

There may be
several reasons
why your fa-
ther is upset. If
your dad is on
the short
side him-
self,
he may
have been
teased about
his height when he was
your age or felt that it placed him at a disadvantage in sports. If this is the case, he may have
hoped that his son wouldn't face the same problems.

Regardless of how tall your father is, he's
probably very aware that in our culture there are
real advantages to being a tall man. All other
things being equal, tall men are often considered
to be more attractive, more likable, and more ca-
pable than shorter men. But it's important to remember that there are very few instances in life
where all other things *are* equal and two people

differ *only* in height. And in general, these other qualities—such as character, intelligence, talent, consideration for other people, and just being a good person—are much more important than how tall you are.

There is a drug called growth hormone that can help youngsters who are *abnormally* short grow a little taller. But this drug is intended for children who do not produce enough growth hormone on their own. Children whose bodies make normal amounts of growth hormone do not grow taller if they are treated with the drug. Since you are developing normally, you would not benefit from treatment.

So the best thing you can do is to concentrate on making the most of the many other things you have going for you and try not to worry about how tall you will eventually be.

By the way, you might be interested in knowing that there are many famous men who obviously haven't found it a disadvantage to be short. The average height of adult men in this country is five feet, nine inches. That means that Sylvester Stallone (5 ft., 7 in.), filmmaker Spike Lee (5 ft., 6 in.), and NBA player Muggsy Bogues (5 ft., 3 in.) of the Golden State Warriors are all examples of men who are "on the short side."

> *"My penis is crooked! When I get an erection, it bends to the left. Why isn't it straight, like in all the pictures I see?"*

There are a wide variety of perfectly normal erections, not just the types that are shown for the sake of illustration. Many penises are straight when erect, but some curve in one direction or another. Also, some penises point directly up when erect, others stand out at right angles to the body, and many are somewhere in between. All these different erections work equally well.

WHICH WAY
DID THEY GO?
THANKS!

> *"Why do my balls shrivel up and get smaller when I'm cold?"*

You may have noticed that your testicles and scrotum get smaller and pull in closer to your body when you get cold and hang lower and farther away from your body when you are hot or have a fever. That's simply your body's way of keeping your sperm at the right temperature. In fact, the need to maintain the right temperature for your sperm is the reason your testicles are outside your body in the first place.

Since the temperature necessary for making sperm is slightly lower than your body temperature, your testicles are placed outside the body, where air circulating around them can keep them cooler. If you become hot, your scrotum hangs even lower and farther away from your body. But if your testicles become too cold, they need your body heat to warm up. So they pull in closer to your torso.

"Sometimes, my cousin and I masturbate together when no one's home. I've read that this is what gay guys do. Does that mean I'm a homosexual?"

It is not unusual for a boy to watch another boy masturbate or to masturbate with a group of boys. Nor is it unusual for two boys to masturbate each other. By itself, this does not mean that you are a homosexual or that you will grow up to be gay.

Homosexuals are men and women who are sexually attracted to people of their own sex, rather than to people of the opposite sex. If, when you are an adult, you find that you are primarily interested in having sexual experiences with other men, you will be considered gay. But when boys and girls are going through puberty, many first explore their bodies and sexual feelings with someone of their own sex. Taking part in this kind of "sex play," as it is called, does not determine whether you will be a heterosexual or homosexual as an adult.

"I've got these light-colored streaks running up and down my butt. My skin is pretty dark, so they really show up. My mom says they're stretch marks, but I thought only pregnant

women got those! What are these things, and how do I get them to go away?"

Anyone—male or female—can get stretch marks. These lines may appear wherever the skin has grown very rapidly and lost some of its elasticity. Being pregnant is certainly one example, but another very common cause is the growth spurt that occurs with puberty. Girls frequently develop stretch marks on their breasts at this time, and they usually aren't any happier about them than you are about yours. Boys and girls who suddenly shoot up in height may also find stretch marks on their legs or torso. And rapid weight gain can cause stretch marks anywhere on the body.

There's nothing you can do to make stretch marks go away, but they usually fade and become less noticeable with time.

"I'm very tall, but my penis and testicles are still real small. What's wrong with me?"

Chances are there's nothing wrong with you, but it's hard to answer this question without knowing how old you are and what you mean by "real small." If you're twelve years old and your testicles have not begun to grow, you probably haven't started puberty yet.

On the other hand, perhaps your testicles are beginning to grow, but not as much as you think they should. It may help to measure your testicles with the orchidometer diagram on page 31. If they've reached the size of the fourth oval, then you have started puberty—you just aren't maturing as fast as you'd like. In this case, it helps to keep in mind that boys who go through puberty at a slower rate still mature eventually.

However, there are some medical problems that can interfere with a boy's development. Generally, if you're fifteen years old and have not experienced *any* of the genital changes discussed in chapter 2, you should see a doctor.

But there doesn't have to be something the matter with you for you to talk with a physician.

Simply being concerned is reason enough. Although a book like this is helpful, no book can answer your individual questions the way a doctor can. And it can be a big relief to know for sure that everything is OK with your own particular body.

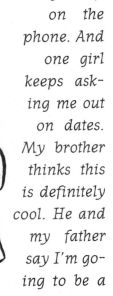

"Since I started sixth grade, all sorts of girls have been calling me up on the phone. And one girl keeps asking me out on dates. My brother thinks this is definitely cool. He and my father say I'm going to be a real stud! But I don't want to be a stud and I don't want to go on a date. Why can't I just do things with the guys like always?"

There's no reason at all why you can't! Just because some of the kids in your class have started going out on dates or hanging out with the opposite sex doesn't mean that you're ready to do this. You may not have control over the rate at which your body matures, but your interests and the things you enjoy doing are still up to you—so take your time.

Both boys and girls can be under a lot of pressure to start becoming interested in the opposite sex. Usually, that pressure comes from other kids. But parents can place subtle pressures on you too, such as expecting you to be glad that girls like you when you couldn't care less. You may be relieved to know that many boys and girls feel exactly the way you do, although some kids are afraid to admit it because they don't want to be considered weird.

CHAPTER 9

"What If . . . ?"

In addition to worrying whether they are developing normally, many boys are concerned that something may go wrong with their bodies in the future. Others wonder what to do if they are faced with some of the difficult situations that can confront boys your age.

If you've had some "What if . . . ?" worries, you may find the answers in this chapter. If not, try to talk over your concerns with your father, your uncle, or another older man you are comfortable with. They probably had some of the same questions when they were younger and will be glad to help you.

"What if I have an erection when I'm giving a report in front of my class?"

Having an erection when you don't want to—especially when it occurs in front of a lot of people—can be very embarrassing. While there's not much you can do to make an erection go away, there are some things you should know that may help you feel less embarrassed. First, you're not alone. This happens to virtually every male at least once in his life. Second—and more important—while you may think it looks as if you have a tent pole in your pants, chances are that others haven't even noticed. Remember, most people are busy looking at your face, not your crotch. And even if they should glance down, your clothes do a pretty good job of concealing an erection.

"My aunt and uncle can't have kids. My mom says they're infertile. Does this run in families? What if this happens to me?"

Infertility, or difficulty in having children, can be caused by many things, but it is not something that is inherited.

In about 40 percent of couples who are infertile, the problem in conceiving a child can be traced to the woman; in another 40 percent, the problem lies with the man. In the remaining couples, both the man and the woman may have problems that contribute to infertility, or both may seem normal but the couple still cannot conceive.

In men, infertility is usually the result of too few sperm or sperm that aren't active enough. Sometimes this problem can be overcome by using medical techniques to accumulate enough active sperm and then placing the sperm inside the woman.

There can be many causes of infertility in women. For example, some women have difficulty ovulating, or releasing mature eggs. In others, infections have caused scars in the fallopian tubes that block eggs from traveling to the uterus. You may remember from chapter 4, that as a woman gets older, she produces fewer and fewer eggs, until finally she stops ovulating completely. This means that women often have more difficulty conceiving after age thirty or thirty-five.

In addition to being able to conceive, a woman must be able to carry a baby until it is developed enough to live outside her body. Some women are able to conceive but then miscarry, giving birth when the baby is much too young to survive.

In recent years, there have been many medical advances that have made it possible for infertile couples to have children. However, it is still easier to avoid some of the things that cause infertility than to treat the problem after it has occurred. For example, left untreated, sexually transmitted diseases such as syphilis, gonorrhea, and chlamydia can result in infertility. That's one reason why it's so important to see a doctor if you suspect you might have one of these infections.

"What if I'm having sex with a girl and I accidentally pee in her?"

A lot of guys wonder if a man can accidentally urinate inside a woman when ejaculating. Fortunately, nature has designed your body so that can't happen. When a man is about to ejaculate, a valve temporarily seals off the bladder so that no urine can escape.

"My girlfriend and I had sex, and she got pregnant. I think she should get an abortion, but what if she doesn't want to? Can I make her? Will I still have to help support the baby even if I don't want it?"

Whether your girlfriend chooses to have an abortion or to have the baby is completely up to her (or her family, depending on her age). She may consider your wishes, but she doesn't have to. Although this may seem unfair, she is the one who will actually have to go through nine months of pregnancy and then labor, on the one hand, or undergo an abortion, on the other, so the decision is up to her. If she has the baby despite your objections, you will still be legally responsible for contributing to your child's financial support when you become an adult. In short, while a boy and a girl have equal say and responsibility in using birth control, if she becomes pregnant, your equal say stops but your equal responsibility does not. It can be very difficult to have decisions about something that will affect the rest of your life in the hands of someone else. Using effective birth control is one way to make sure this doesn't happen.

> "My dad left my mother last year. Now he's living with another man. It doesn't bother him if people know he's gay, but it bothers me! What if my friends find out? Will they think I'm gay too?"

Children often find it difficult to cope with a parent's announcement that he or she is homosexual. Many kids in this situation fear that their friends will think they are gay too and will not want to be around them. Sometimes they also worry about whether or not this means they will grow up to be homosexual themselves. That's why it's important for you to know that your parents' sexuality does not determine what yours will be. There is no evidence that children of homosexuals are more likely to be gay than children of heterosexuals.

Rather than hide the fact that they have a gay parent, some children choose to tell their friends. This has two advantages. First, you don't have to worry about pretending anymore, at least with the people you confide in. And second, you have some control over when and what your friends are told.

If you do decide to tell some of your friends, it's a good idea to choose carefully before sharing this information. Be sure the person is a good and trustworthy friend, not someone who will see this as an opportunity to spread gossip. Also, remember that *how* you tell your friends has a great deal to do with their reaction. If you act as if you are sharing a horrible, shameful secret, they are likely to feel the same way. But if you are matter-of-fact and say something like, "My dad is gay, but he's still a great dad and I love him," then your friends will probably think it's no big deal.

"Until I was in the eighth grade, I was really great at sports. But now I'm not any good at all! What happened to me? What if I'm like this forever? Is there anything I can do to get back to the way I was?"

Chances are that you've grown a lot recently. If so, it's no surprise that your body doesn't seem to respond as well as it did before. It takes time for your brain to learn how to get your new arms, legs, feet, and hands to work together. Therefore, many adolescents go through a period of being clumsy. Not surprisingly, this awkwardness is

most noticeable in activities that require a lot of coordination, like sports. Although it's hard, try to be patient. In a little while, your body will start to pull together again, and you'll probably find that your athletic ability has returned.

> "I met this great girl on the Internet. Her family is going to be visiting my hometown next month, and she wants me to meet them at the zoo. That's near my house, so I could go right after school. But what if I don't like her when I meet her in person?"

It can be a lot of fun to meet people on-line. It's a chance to get to know kids from different parts of the country and to talk to those who are interested in the same things you are. But despite the good things about the Internet, there are some serious risks in meeting people there. So you are right to be hesitant about getting together with your on-line friend in person.

Perhaps the biggest problem with meeting people on-line is that you have no way of knowing whether they are who they say they are. For example, occasionally, a forty-year-old man may

pretend to be a twelve-year-old girl or a fourteen-year-old boy in order to meet young kids. As you can guess, there's something very wrong with a middle-aged man who wants to meet children this way. Unfortunately, people like this can be very good at faking their identity, so it is hard to spot them.

However, by following a few simple rules, you can help to make sure that your on-line friendships are safe. First, get your parents' permission before sharing any personal information about you or your family—such as your address, your telephone number, your parents' work address or phone number, or even the name and location of your school. Also get their permission before sending your friends a picture of you. Even if on-line friends send you their photos, keep in mind that these might not really be pictures of them.

Never agree to get together with an on-line friend without first checking with your parents. Even if your parents say it's OK, ask them to come with you the first time and arrange to meet in a public place. That way, you can all get to know each other in safe surroundings. Even if your friend is actually who she says she is, your parents can help you make a polite excuse for leaving early if it turns out that you and she don't get along in person.

There are a few other tips to remember when going on-line, as well. Do not answer any messages you may get that are mean, threatening, or make you uncomfortable, and let your parents know that you've received them. It's not your fault if you get messages like this, and the people who send them are abusing you and the Internet. Finally, you and your parents should set up some family rules about the time of day and the length of time when you can be on-line. Then stick to these rules.

"Last month I got kicked really hard in the balls during soccer practice. The other guys laughed, but it hurt so much I couldn't even breathe. What if my testicles are ruined? Even if they're not, I'm scared to go back to practice. What if it happens again?"

Being hit in the testicles is one of the most agonizing experiences a male can have. In fact, even seeing another male in this extremely vulnerable and painful situation makes most guys feel helpless and afraid. Laughter is one means of pushing away their anxiety and fear.

It can be hard to imagine that something so painful hasn't seriously injured you. But in almost all cases, being hit in the testicles does not cause permanent damage. However, if you continue to feel pain or notice anything unusual in your testicles following this or any other injury, you should talk to your doctor.

It's understandable that you want to avoid situations in which this could happen again, but that's hard to do if you want to lead a regular life. However, you can take steps to reduce the risk of getting hurt. For example, it's a good idea to wear an athletic protector when playing any contact sport.

"There's some weird stuff going on in the men's room at the movies in my town. When a friend of mine was in there, a man offered him money to feel his penis. My friend got scared and ran. What should I do if this happens to me?"

Exactly what your friend did.

It should be a simple matter to use a public bathroom, but unfortunately, these places are not always as safe as they should be. If you feel uncomfortable in a public bathroom for *any reason,* trust your instincts and leave. This can be hard if you really have to pee, but you can always try to come back a little later. By then, the person who made you uncomfortable may have left or there may be other people in the bathroom, which will help you feel safer. If someone actually asks you to do something that you don't want to, say no and leave. If you can, try to tell one of the movie employees what happened. And finally, if anyone grabs you or tries to keep you from leaving, scream, yell, and make as much noise as you can. You don't need to be embarrassed; you're not the one doing something wrong.

"What if my penis gets caught in my zipper?"

This happens more often than you might think. And, when it does, it can really hurt! The loose skin of the scrotum is more likely than the skin of the penis to get caught in your zipper, but the procedure for getting it out is the same. First, try not to panic. Pull the zipper back as gently as possible until the skin is free. (This will probably sting some, but hang in there.)

As soon as you've untangled yourself from the zipper, try to put ice on the injured area. This will help keep swelling down. To prevent infection, you should also apply an antibiotic ointment to any place where the skin has been cut. Ordinarily, these steps are enough to keep any further problems from occurring. However, if you have continued swelling or notice signs of infection, you should see a doctor.

Obviously, this is an experience you don't want to repeat. Since it generally happens when a person is in a hurry and not really paying attention, slow down a little when zipping up your pants, particularly if you aren't wearing underwear.

CHAPTER 10

"If I'd Known Then What I Know Now!"

Have you ever wished you could go back and re-live a difficult time in your life now that you've gotten smarter? Of course, none of us can do that. But the fifteen men interviewed in this chapter hoped you might benefit from some of the things they didn't learn until they were older. Although their ages range from twenty-six to sixty-two, they had a lot of the same concerns when they were adolescents. Here are some of the changes they would have made if they had known then what they know now.

Most of these guys remember feeling insecure when they were teenagers. If they could do it all over again, many would try to handle these feelings differently.

Kevin: I wish I'd been able to just accept myself—the good and the bad. Sometimes, it's the things that aren't so perfect about you that make it possible for you to get closer to other people.

Jim: I remember adolescence mostly as a fog of self-consciousness. If I had known how little notice people take of other people's flaws and how little it matters when they do, my teen years would have been much less painful.

For others, lack of information affected how they felt about themselves or made adolescence much more difficult than necessary.

Brad: I was the only person in my group of friends who wasn't circumcised, and I always wondered why I was different. I didn't know they'd all had their foreskins removed when they were babies. I wish I'd had someone I could have asked about this, and I wish I'd known that it doesn't matter whether you're circumcised or not.

Ron: I wish I'd known more about the changes of adolescence. As a quiet person, I couldn't ask others for feedback. I didn't try out for a lot of things, like sports, because I was insecure and afraid of making a fool of myself. I think if I had understood the changes I was going through, I would have been a lot more confident.

Steve: I don't think any of the guys I knew thought that masturbating would make you go blind or grow hair on your palms. But I, for one, believed it made acne worse. And any pain I had in my abdomen or groin, I attributed to masturbating. It's lucky I never had appendicitis. I probably would have died, trying to keep it a secret.

Knowing that things change with time would have been reassuring.

Ron: I also wish I'd understood that the way I was at the time didn't mean that I would always be that way. Adolescents tend to measure themselves by what

they can't do. They don't take into account that intellectual and physical development are uneven. They think, "Once a geek, always a geek." It's important not to let others label you—or to label yourself—based on how you are at the moment, because things change. But labels tend to make things feel permanent.

Others felt that some of the things they know now would have helped them handle the pressures of adolescence better.

Eric: I wish I'd known that it's OK to be an individual, to not go along with the pack. And I wish I'd known it's OK to walk away from a dare.

Kevin: I wish I'd known that it's OK not to know what you want to be when you get out of school. And that even if you do, it's OK to change your mind later. Knowing that would have taken a lot of pressure off me.

> *Almost all wish they had known more about girls—what a female's body is like, what makes girls tick, and how to act around them. And if these men could relive their adolescence, they would definitely change some of the ideas they had about sex.*

David: I would have liked to have had the ability not to get hurt as easily as I did with respect to girls. I thought they were some type of magical beings. Now I know they had some of the same problems I was having.

Tom: I would have liked to have had some

knowledge about feelings on a first date. I was so scared and had no confidence. I wish that I'd known that the girl was just as scared as I was.

Jerry: I wish I'd known that there was a lot more to life than sex, and that I had a lot of time to get sexually involved. I would have been more interested in girls with higher morals. I wouldn't be as shy because now I know that the girls were shy too.

Neville: I wish I'd had a chance to see some pictures of what females' bodies look like. As a teenager, I had heard they had pubic hair, but I wasn't sure. I asked a girl I was dating if I could look at her down there. I didn't have a flashlight, so while we were in the backseat of the car fooling around, I lit a couple of matches to try to see her pubic area. I saw it all right, but I accidentally burned her.

Don: I wish I'd known I could have been a lot more aggressive with girls—but I don't want any of my daughter's friends to hear that!

Matt: I wish I'd had more courage as a teenager. I would have been braver in pursuing girls. I was really shy and wouldn't take the

chance of being turned down. I know now that being turned down wouldn't have killed me. "Nothing ventured, nothing gained," would be my philosophy if I had it to do over.

Larry: If I could live my life over, I'd like to have the ability to really figure females out. I've learned that what they say isn't always what they mean.

Ron: I wish I'd realized that most of what my friends said they were doing sexually was nothing but a bluff. It put a lot of pressure on me to have sex and distorted how I saw girls. There was always this sense that the only thing that was important about you was the number of females you could rattle off. The one thing almost every man wishes he had known is that it's not about performance. All that energy spent trying to be the greatest sexually has made more men more miserable that anything else.

John: I wish I'd realized that I had the rest of

my life to get seriously involved with a girl. I would have played the field more.

Charlie: I'd know not to get so serious with a girl so quickly.

Steve: With the physical changes of puberty, it seemed that girls turned into alien beings, instead of people just like us. While my friends and I spent countless hours speculating about how girls thought and what they were planning to do, it never occurred to us that they shared the same aspirations, desires, and insecurities that we did. I wish I'd known that the best guide to how a girl might feel about something was to put myself in that situation and see how I'd feel.

You'll be happy to know that all these guys not only survived puberty but went on to become happy and successful men. Still, it's always easier if you have someone you can talk to about your concerns, instead of having to learn everything the hard way. Just as the men above were eager to share their experiences with you, your father or other males such as your uncles and coaches will probably be glad to answer your questions too. All you have to do is ask.

Index

changing, 46–61
growth spurt, 20–21
having sex, 69
interest in, 118–19
knowledge about, 139–43
Gonorrhea, 92–93, 94, 123
Growth hormone, 112
Growth spurt, 20–22, 116
in girls, 48–49

Hair, 2, 16–20, 24, 50
Having sex, 62–72
admitting to parents, 98
decision regarding, 64
with HIV-infected
partner, 102
homosexuals, 71
postponing, 99
pressure regarding,
66–70
readiness for, 66–68
Height, 1, 20, 110–13
girls, 48–49
Herpes, 93
Heterosexuals, 70, 71, 72, 115
Homosexuality/homosexu-
als, 70–72, 114, 115
parents, 125–26
Hormonal changes
and menstruation, 60–61

Hormones, 11, 41, 81
Human immunodeficiency
virus (HIV), 100–103
Human immunodeficiency
virus (HIV) infection
preventing, 104–6
treating, 103–4

Infertility, 92, 122–23
Inner lips, 53
Insecurity, 135–36, 137
Internet, 128–30
IUDs, 83, 86, 87

Lee, Spike, 112–13

Maleness, 2, 3
Masturbation, 45–47,
114–15, 137
Menstruation, 56–61, 79, 81
bleeding in, 59–60
pain in, 58–59
Mothers, 109
Multiple births, 77
Muscular development, 1,
22
Mustache, 17, 19

Needles, sharing, 102, 103,
105

Public bathrooms,
    encounters in, 132–33

Race, 14, 16, 19
Rape, 69
Razor bumps, 20
Reproduction, 3, 10
Rhythm method, 78–80,
    87

Scarring, 25
Scrotum, 4–5, 110
    changing, 11, 13
    effect of cold and heat
        on, 114
    warts on, 95
Semen, 37, 41, 44, 83, 94,
    100, 102
Seminal vesicles, 7, 41
Sex, taking care in, 106–7
    see also Having sex
Sex play, 115
Sexual intercourse, 46
    pain during, 97
Sexual performance, 142
Sexual stimulation, 38–39,
    41
Sexually transmitted
    diseases (STDs),
    90–107, 123

preventing, 99–100
warning signs of,
    96–97
Shaving, 19–20
    girls, 50
Skin changes, 23–25
Sperm, 3, 4–5, 37, 44,
    46, 55, 78, 79, 80,
    122
    joining egg, 56, 73–75
    placing in woman's
        body, 55–56
    temperature for, 114
    traveling from testicles
        to penis, 6–7, 40–41
Sexual organs, 3
    external, 4
    internal, 4, 5
    see also Genitals
Spermicides, 82, 83, 84,
    85
Stallone, Sylvester,
    112–13
STDs
    see Sexually transmitted
        diseases
Stretch marks, 115–16
Sweat glands, 27, 28, 50,
    110
Syphilis, 91–93, 94, 123